LONDON COLLEGE OF MUSIC

Grade Six

Classical Guitar Playing

Compiled by
Tony Skinner, Raymond Burley and Amanda Cook
on behalf of

RGT®
Registry of Guitar Tutors

Printed and bound in Great Britain

A CIP record for this publication is available from the British Library
ISBN: 978-1-905908-16-5

Published by Registry Publications

Registry Mews, Wilton Rd, Bexhill, Sussex, TN40 1HY

Cover artwork by Danielle Croft. Design by JAK Images.
Music engraving by Alan J Brown, Chaz Hart and Dmitry Milovanov.

Compiled for **LCM Exams** by

INTRODUCTION

This publication is part of a progressive series of ten handbooks, primarily intended for candidates considering taking the London College Of Music examinations in classical guitar playing. However, given each handbook's wide content of musical repertoire and associated educational material, the series provides a solid foundation of musical education for any classical guitar student – whether intending to take an examination or not. Whilst the handbooks can be used for independent study, they are ideally intended as a supplement to individual or group tuition.

Examination entry

An examination entry form is provided at the rear of each handbook. This is the only valid entry form for the London College Of Music classical guitar examinations.

Please note that *if the entry form is detached and lost, it will not be replaced under any circumstances* and the candidate will be required to obtain a replacement handbook to obtain another entry form.

Editorial information

Examination performances must be from this handbook edition. All performance pieces should be played in full, including all repeats shown; the pieces have been edited specifically for examination use, with all non-required repeat markings omitted. Tempos, fingering and dynamic markings are for general guidance only and need not be rigidly adhered to, providing an effective musical result is achieved. In some pieces such markings are kept to a minimum to allow candidates to display individual interpretation; the omission of editorial dynamic markings does not in any way imply that dynamic variation should be absent from a performance.

Pick-hand fingering is normally shown on the stem side of the notes:
p = thumb; *i* = index finger; *m* = middle finger; *a* = third finger.

Fret-hand fingering is shown with the numbers **1 2 3 4**, normally to the left of the notehead. **0** indicates an open string.

String numbers are shown in a circle, normally below the note. For example, ⑥ = 6th string.

Finger-shifts are indicated by a small horizontal dash before the left-hand finger number.

For example, **2** followed by **-2** indicates that the 2nd finger can stay on the same string but move to another fret as a *guide finger*. The finger-shift sign should not be confused with a *slide* or *glissando* (where a longer dash joins two noteheads).

Slurs are indicated by a curved line between two notes of differing pitch. These should not be confused with *ties* (where two notes of the same pitch are joined by a curved line in order to increase the duration of the first note).

Full barrés (covering 5 or 6 strings with the first finger) are shown by a capital B, followed by a Roman numeral to indicate the fret position of the barré. *Half barrés* (covering 2 to 4 strings) are shown like this: ½B, followed by a Roman numeral to indicate the fret position of the half barré. For example, ½BI indicates a half barré at the first fret. A dotted line will indicate the duration for which the barré should be held.

Harmonics are shown with a diamond-shaped notehead. The fret at which they are to be played will be shown above each note, e.g. H12 for 12th fret, and the string number will be shown. On the stave, harmonics are generally placed at the pitch of the fretted note above which they are played – rather than the pitch at which they sound.

Arpeggiated chords, that are rolled or strummed, are indicated by a vertical wavy line to the left of the chord.

TECHNICAL WORK

 maximum of 15 marks may be awarded in this section of the examination. The examiner may ask the candidate to play *from memory* any of the scales, arpeggios or chords shown on the following pages.

- The following two octave scales may be requested in *any* key: major, harmonic and melodic minor.
- The following chords and arpeggios may be requested at *any* pitch: major, minor and dominant 7th.
- All requirements that are specified as 'in any key' are shown overleaf with 'transpositional' patterns, i.e. they can be transposed to other pitches by using the same finger pattern starting from a different fret.

Where a transpositional pattern is written in C it can be transposed along the fifth string by starting on the following frets: 4th fret for C♯/D♭, 5th fret for D, 6th fret for D♯/E♭, 7th fret for E, 8th fret for F, 9th fret for F♯/G♭.

Where a transpositional pattern is written in G it can be transposed along the sixth string by starting on the following frets: 4th fret for G♯/A♭, 5th fret for A, 6th fret for A♯/B♭, 7th fret for B.

Scales and arpeggios should be played *ascending and descending*, i.e. from the lowest note to the highest and back again, without a pause and without repeating the top note. It is recommended that arpeggios and double-stopped scales are played *tirando* (i.e. using free strokes) and that all other scales are played *apoyando* (i.e. using rest strokes), although tirando can be used providing a good tone is produced. Any effective and systematic combination of alternating fingers may be used to pick the strings.

Chords should be played *ascending only*, and sounded string by string, starting with the lowest root note. To achieve a legato sound, the whole chord shape should be placed on the fingerboard before, and kept on during, playing. Chords should always be played tirando, i.e. using free strokes. The following right-hand fingering is recommended for chords: *p* for all bass strings, *ima* for the treble strings.

To allow for flexibility in teaching and playing approaches, all the fingering suggestions within this handbook are not compulsory and alternative systematic fingerings, that are musically effective, will be accepted. Suggested tempos are for general guidance only. Slightly slower or faster performances will be acceptable, providing that the tempo is maintained evenly throughout.

Recommended tempo	
Scales:	132 minim beats per minute
Double-stopped scales:	66 minim beats per minute
Arpeggios:	96 minim beats per minute
Chords:	132 minim beats per minute

Key Study

The Key Study links the introduction of a new key to the performance of a short melodic theme from a piece by a well-known composer. The purpose is to make the learning of scales relevant to practical music-making and therefore memorable, as well as providing the opportunity to play music outside the standard guitar repertoire.

The examiner may request you to play any, or all, of the scales within the Key Study. The examiner will also ask for a performance of ONE of the melodic themes of your choice.

Tempo markings and fingering are for guidance only and need not be rigidly adhered to, providing a good musical performance is produced. The examiner will be listening, and awarding marks, for evidence of melodic phrasing and shaping, as well as for accuracy and clarity.

The Key Study must be played entirely from memory.

C Major scale - 2 octaves (Transpositional pattern)

G Major scale - 2 octaves (Transpositional pattern)

C Harmonic Minor scale - 2 octaves (Transpositional pattern)

G Harmonic Minor scale - 2 octaves (Transpositional pattern)

C Melodic Minor scale - 2 octaves (Transpositional pattern)

G Melodic Minor scale - 2 octaves (Transpositional pattern)

F Chromatic scale - 3 octaves

F Major scale - 3 octaves

F Harmonic Minor scale - 3 octaves

F Melodic Minor scale - 3 octaves

C Major scale - 1 octave in 3rds   **C Major scale - 1 octave in 6ths**

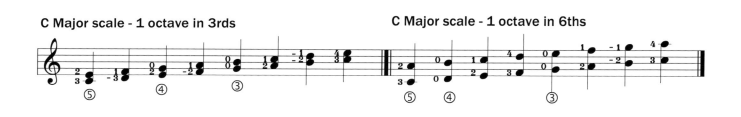

C Major scale - 1 octave in 8ths   **C Major scale - 1 octave in 10ths**

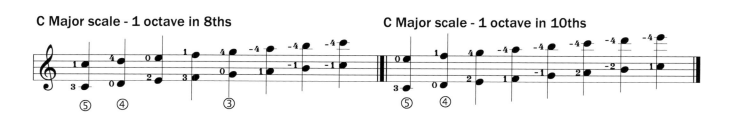

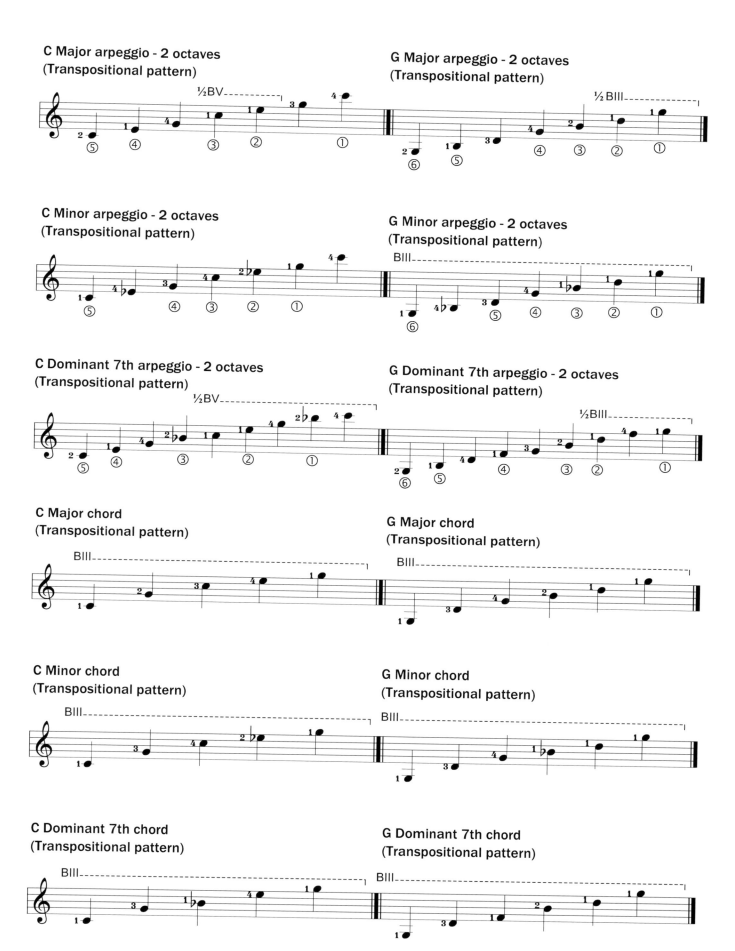

Key Study

The examiner will request a selection of the scales below,
plus ONE melodic theme *of the candidate's choice.*

B Major scale - 2 octaves

G# Harmonic Minor scale - 2 octaves

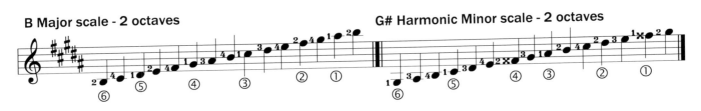

G# Melodic Minor scale - 2 octaves

Melodic theme - Option One

Rondeau
From Abdelazar

Henry Purcell
(1659 - 1695)

♩ = 69

Melodic theme - Option Two

Jupiter
From The Planets Suite

Gustav Holst
(1874 - 1934)

PERFORMANCE

C andidates should play *three* pieces. The programme should be balanced, with some contrasting pieces to demonstrate the candidate's range. At least two of the pieces must be chosen from those included in this handbook; the third piece can also be from the handbook *or*, if preferred, it can be either a 'free choice' piece of the candidate's own choosing – providing it is of at least a similar technical level to the pieces in this handbook, or it can be a piece taken from the supplementary list shown in the LCM Exams Repertoire List for this grade (viewable via the RGT website www.RegistryOfGuitarTutors.com or obtainable from LCM Exams).

Performance Tips

The performance notes below are intended to provide helpful advice and information, however candidates are free to present alternative technical solutions and musical interpretations – providing that a musically effective and stylistically appropriate result is achieved.

Preludium *(Dowland)*:

This piece was originally written for the lute by John Dowland. It was not intended as an introduction to another piece. Dowland is the most renowned lutenist of all time. He lived in England, but travelled widely in Europe and was even appointed as lutenist to the King of Denmark. Preludium should be played expressively and with no feeling of urgency. Judge your performance tempo by the clarity and control of the demisemiquaver (32nd note) passages that appear later in the piece.

Bourée *(J.S. Bach)*:

German composer Johann Sebastian Bach was best known during his lifetime as a highly respected organist. Today he is recognised worldwide as one of the foremost composers of all time, particularly for his skilled use of contrapuntal writing. This Bourée is the penultimate movement from his first Lute Suite, written in the first quarter of the 18th century. The title 'Bourée' refers to the name of a dance of French origin. All Bourées contain certain similar characteristics in that they have: two main pulses to the bar; all main phrases begin on the last crotchet of a bar; and the music is divided into two sections.

This Bourée is a fine example of Bach's skill in the use of counterpoint. A good exercise is to play through just the bass line of this piece before you attempt the whole work. As the second section involves a much greater level of fingerboard movement than the first section, it is advisable to choose the starting tempo very carefully – selecting a speed that can be maintained throughout.

Canarios *(Sanz)*:

Canarios was written for the five-course (baroque) guitar and is a lively Spanish dance, possibly originating in the Canary Islands. Although the piece has a $\frac{6}{8}$ time signature you will notice many bars in $\frac{3}{4}$. Be careful to perform the rhythms accurately. Like all Sanz's pieces the original is written in tablature. The short double bar lines, included from the tablature, indicate the end of a section (which may also have been used as a repeat point). Many of the left hand slurs are editorial. The pairs of chords towards the end of the piece should be strummed in alternate directions: downstroke (with the thumb or index finger), followed by an upstroke with the index finger.

Maestoso *(Giuliani)*:

Mauro Giuliani was born in Italy and later lived in Austria. He was one of the greatest guitar virtuosos of his day, as well as a prolific composer. In this piece the melody notes marked with tenuto lines should be held and slightly emphasised. The semiquaver octave lines need particular attention to avoid fretbuzz: as fret widths get progressively smaller on the higher reaches of the fingerboard, the left-hand span will need to constrict or expand according to the fret position.

Allegro *(Carcassi)*:

Born in Italy, Matteo Carcassi later made France his home. As a virtuoso performer on the guitar Carcassi regularly toured Europe. He wrote much music for the guitar, including many studies and a successful guitar teaching method. This piece forms part of his popular collection, 25 Melodic And Progressive Studies Opus 60. The piece involves much fingerboard movement, however this can nearly always be facilitated by the use of an open string to mask the change of position. A good example of this is in bar 2, where use of the open E string enables a smooth transition between 9th and 1st position.

Rosita *(Tárrega)*:

Spanish guitarist Francisco Tárrega is often called 'the father of the modern classical guitar' due to his great influence on expanding its technique and repertoire. The sub-title of this piece, Polka, suggests a lively dance (originating from Bohemia) with a strong two-in-the-bar feel. The numerous slide signs should be observed as they add a light-hearted touch, so forming an integral part of the music, and are typical in Tárrega's writing.

Preludio Tristón *(M.D.Pujol)*:

The Argentinean composer Maximo Diego Pujol is not to be confused with the Spanish composer Emilio Pujol. Preludio Triston (Sad Prelude) is the second from a set of five preludes. The Tempo di Milonga direction indicates that the piece should be performed in the time, or speed, of a Milonga – this is a musical genre, or dance, not dissimilar to a slow, sultry tango. The notation in this handbook version is taken directly from the publisher's manuscript edited by John W. Duarte, and slurs are indicated by a series of dots forming a dotted curved line. The notes towards the end of the piece, that are indicated to be played an octave higher, should be performed using artificial harmonics.

Jono *(Skinner)*:

This piece by British guitarist and music educator Tony Skinner should be played in a free and dreamy way, with much use of rubato. Notes within each bar should be held on to form chord shapes wherever possible. This piece has been notated using a contemporary notational style with unified stem directions for ease of reading, rather than in the traditional two-voice notational format. The tempo should be slow and never rushed. The timbre should be warm throughout; the left hand fingering has been chosen specifically to facilitate this.

Preludium

John Dowland
(1563 - 1626)

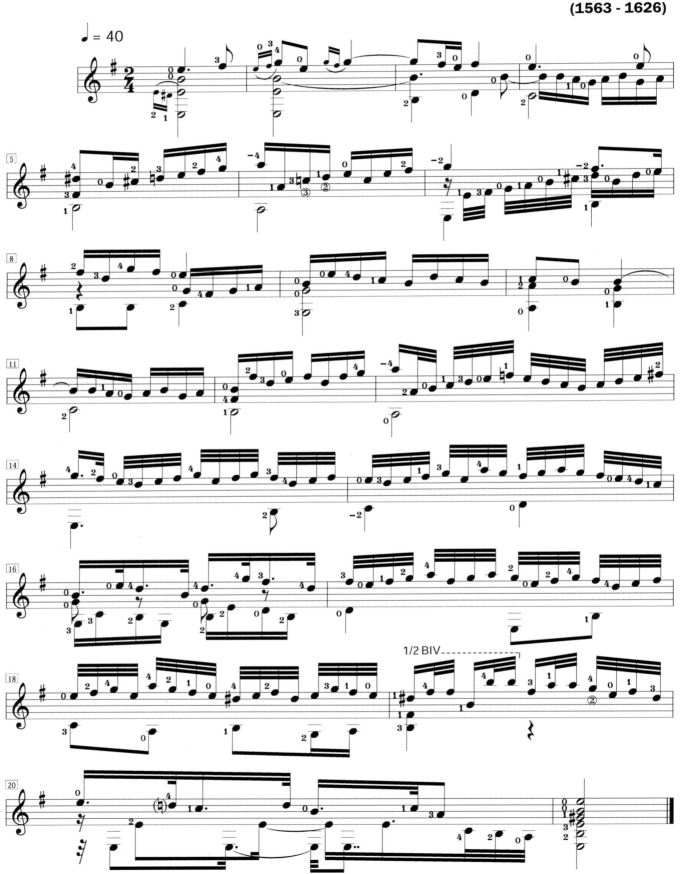

12

Bourée

Johann Sebastian Bach
(1685 - 1750)

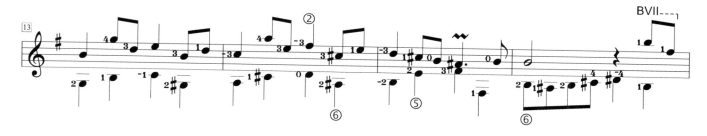

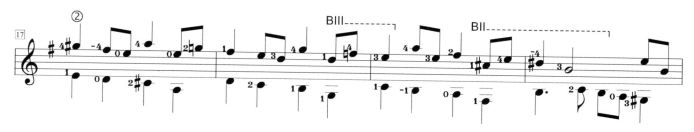

13

Canarios

Gaspar Sanz
(1640 - 1710)

Maestoso Op.48 No.13

Mauro Giuliani
(1781 - 1829)

Allegro Op.60 No.23

Matteo Carcassi
(1792 - 1853)

17

Rosita

Francisco Tárrega
(1852 - 1909)

18

Preludio Tristón

Máximo Diego Pujol
(1957 –)

♩ = 72

Tempo di Milonga

19

Jono

Tony Skinner
(1960 –)

VIVA VOCE

I n this section of the examination candidates will be engaged in a short discussion to enable the examiner to assess the candidate's understanding of musical fundamentals and their responses to the pieces played. A maximum of 7 marks may be awarded.

At this grade candidates should be able to:

- explain the meaning of all notational elements in the music performed in the Performance component of the exam;

- identify intervals up to and including an octave by number and type (e.g. 'Major 7th', 'Perfect 5th', etc.);

- identify major and minor chords as occurring in the music (either as chords or as melodic patterns);

- identify melodic and harmonic features of the music (e.g. modulations, sequence, melodic inversion, circle of 5ths, pedal points, etc.);

- demonstrate knowledge of formal structures (e.g. binary, ternary, etc.);

- identify the historical period of the music performed (Renaissance, Baroque, etc.) and demonstrate background knowledge of the composers;

- demonstrate a basic understanding of the workings of the guitar and name its principal constituent parts;

- describe the mood and character of pieces using appropriate descriptive terminology and identify contrasts of mood within pieces and describe any pictorial or descriptive element of the music;

- discuss their personal responses to the music performed, i.e. the extent to which they like or dislike it, or find it challenging or rewarding, and why;

- discuss their approaches to learning the pieces including the use of certain techniques, aspects of interpretation and identifying any particular difficulties (musical or technical) that were encountered;

- demonstrate a self-critical awareness of their own performance, indicating to the examiner which aspects of their performance they were happy or unhappy with and why.

Potential candidates lacking knowledge in this general area are advised to study for the London College of Music Theory of Music examinations, using suitable music theory books, worksheets and musical dictionaries. Advice and tuition from an experienced teacher would undoubtedly prove most advantageous.

Below are some examples of the *type* of questions that the examiner may ask at this grade - although the overall number of questions will not be as extensive as all the examples given below. Note that these are examples only; the list is by no means exhaustive. The wording and phrasing of the questions may vary even when the same topic is involved. The examiner's questions will be limited to one or more of the pieces performed.

At this level, specimen answers are deliberately not supplied in order to encourage candidates to undertake broader research and to avoid the temptation to learn answers by rote.

Question: What can you tell me about John Dowland?

Question: What is the historical period of *Canarios*?

Question: What key is *Rosita* in, and when does the piece modulate and to what key?

Question: Explain the meaning of the ornament that appears in bar 7 of *Bourée*.

Question: What do the following terms that appear in the *Preludio Tristón* mean?
(a) poco rall. (b) piu mosso (c) ben cantando

Question: What is the interval between the first two notes in *Preludio Tristón*?

Question: Can you identify the chord in bar 8 of *Preludio Tristón*?

Question: Describe the closing cadence in *Maestoso*.

Question: Tell me about the form of Carcassi's *Allegro*.

Question: Identify some of the main melodic or harmonic features of Dowland's *Preludium*.

Question: What do you notice about the melody in bar 13 of Dowland's *Preludium*?

Question: Of the pieces you played today, which is the most challenging piece and why?

Question: How do you think your performance of *Jono* went today?

SIGHT READING _____

The examiner will show you the sight reading test and allow you just a short time to look over it before performing it. The piece will be 8 bars long, and may contain 4 note chords, triplets and syncopated rhythms. The key signature range will be 2 flats to 4 sharps. The fingerboard range will not exceed 5th position. The time signature will be either $\frac{2}{4}$, $\frac{3}{4}$, $\frac{4}{4}$ or $\frac{6}{8}$. Up to 10 marks may be awarded.

SIGHT READING TIPS

1. Always check the key and time signature BEFORE you start to play.

2. Once you have identified the key it is helpful to remember that the notes will all come from the key scale.

3. Before you start to play, quickly scan through the piece and check any chords or rhythms that you are unsure of. Where fretted bass notes occur simultaneously with melody notes, decide which left-hand fingering you will need to use.

4. Note the tempo or style marking, but be careful to play at a tempo at which you can maintain accuracy throughout.

5. Once you start to play, try and keep your eyes on the music. Avoid the temptation to keep looking at the fingerboard – that's a sure way to lose your place in the music.

6. Observe all rests and try to follow the dynamic markings.

7. If you do make an error, try not to let it affect your confidence for the rest of the piece. It is better to keep going and capture the overall shape of the piece, rather than stopping and going back to correct errors.

The following examples show the *type* of pieces that will be presented in the examination.

(i)   Allegretto

(ii)   Larghetto

(iii)   Moderato

(iv)   Allegretto

AURAL TESTS _____

A maximum of 8 marks may be awarded in this section of the examination. The tests will be played by the examiner on either guitar or piano, at the examiner's discretion. The examples below are shown in guitar notation and give a broad indication of the type of tests that will be given during the examination. Candidates wishing to view sample tests in piano notation should obtain the current LCM Exams *Specimen Aural Tests* booklet.

Test 1

The examiner will play a harmonised passage in simple time, of not more than six bars, which may contain some syncopated patterns. After two playings, candidates will be asked to:

(a)   identify the time signature.

(b)   identify whether the passage is in a major or minor key.

(c)   identify, by number and type, any interval within the octave, occurring in the melody line between two succeeding notes. These pitches will be played again, first as occurring in the melody, and then with the pitches sounded together.

(d)   clap or tap back the rhythm of a short phrase from the passage, of 1-2 bars in length, played again in an unharmonised version.

(e)   identify and describe the note values (rhythmic values) in the phrase from (d) above.

Here are two examples.

Test 2a

The candidate will be required to identify either a perfect, imperfect or interrupted cadence by name. The cadence will be played by the examiner in a major key and in the form of two block chords at the end of a short melody. The tonic chord will be played before the test. Here are some examples of the style of test.

Test 2b

The candidate should state into which key a passage has modulated, either by name or by relationship to the home key. Modulations will be restricted to subdominant, dominant and relative minor from a major key opening. The passage may be played up to two times. The tonic chord will be sounded before each playing and the key named. Here are some examples of the style of test.

Subdominant
A major to D major

Dominant
C major to G major

Relative minor
A major to F♯ minor

LONDON COLLEGE OF MUSIC

Classical Guitar
Examination Entry Form
GRADE SIX
or Leisure Play Upper Intermediate

**The standard LCM Exams music entry form is NOT valid for Classical Guitar entries.
Entry to the examination is only possible via this original form.
Photocopies of this form will not be accepted under any circumstances.**

Please use black ink and block capital letters when completing this form.

Circle the type of examination you wish to enter: • Grade examination   • Leisure Play examination.

SESSION (Spring/Summer/Winter): _____ YEAR: _____

Preferred Examination Centre (if known): _____
If left blank you will be examined at the nearest venue to your home address.

Candidate Details:

Candidate Name (as to appear on certificate):

_____

Candidate ID (if entered previously): _____ Date of birth: _____

Gender (M/F): _____ Ethnicity (see chart overleaf): _____

Date of birth and ethnicity details are for statistical purposes only, and are not passed on to the examiner.

☐   Tick this box if you are attaching details of particular needs requirements.

Teacher Details:

Teacher Name (as to appear on certificate): _____

Teacher Qualifications (if required on certificate): _____

LCM Teacher Code (if entered previously): _____

Address: _____

_____ Postcode: _____

Tel. No. (day): _____ (evening): _____

☐   Tick this box if any details above have changed since your last LCM entry.

IMPORTANT NOTES

- It is the candidate's responsibility to have knowledge of, and comply with, the current syllabus requirements. Where candidates are entered for examinations by a teacher, the teacher must take responsibility that candidates are entered in accordance with the current syllabus requirements. Failure to carry out any of the examination requirements may lead to disqualification.

- For candidates with particular needs, a letter giving details and requests for any special requirements (e.g. enlarged sight reading), together with an official supporting document (e.g. medical certificate), should be attached.

- Examinations may be held on any day of the week, including weekends. Any appointment requests (e.g. 'prefer morning,' or 'prefer weekdays') must be made at the time of entry. **LCM Exams and its Representatives will take note of the information given; however, no guarantees can be made that all wishes can be met.**

- Submission of this entry is an undertaking to abide by the current regulations.

ETHNIC ORIGIN CLASSIFICATIONS

White
01   British
02   Irish
03   Other white background

Mixed
04   White and black Caribbean
05   White and black African
06   White and Asian
07   Other mixed background

Asian or Asian British
08   Indian
09   Pakistani
10   Bangladeshi
11   Other Asian background

Black or Black British
12   Caribbean
13   African
14   Other black background

Chinese or Other Ethnic Group
15   Chinese
16   Other

17   **Prefer not to say**

Examination Fee: £ _____

Late Entry Fee (if necessary) £ _____

Total amount submitted: £ _____

Cheques or postal orders should be made payable to *'Thames Valley University'*.

A list of current fees, entry deadlines and session dates is available from LCM Exams.

Where to submit your entry form

Entries for public centres should be sent to the
**LCM Exams local examination centre representative
(NOT to the LCM Exams Head Office).**

View the LCM Exams website http://mercury.tvu.ac.uk/lcmexams
or contact the LCM Exams office (tel: 020 8231 2364 / email: lcm.exams@tvu.ac.uk)
for details of your nearest local examination centre representative.

Entries for the London area only, or for private centres, should be sent direct to:
LCM Exams, Thames Valley University, Walpole House, 18-22 Bond St, London, W5 5AA

Official Entry Form